MW00910872

STANDARDIZED TEST PREPARATION

HARCOURT
science

**California
Edition**

GRADE 2

PUPIL EDITION

Harcourt School Publishers

Orlando • Boston • Dallas • Chicago • San Diego

www.harcourtschool.com

Copyright © by Harcourt, Inc.

All rights reserved. No part of this publication may be reproduced
or transmitted in any form or by any means, electronic or
mechanical, including photocopy, recording, or any information
storage and retrieval system, without permission in writing from
the publisher.

Requests for permission to make copies of any part of the work
should be mailed to the following address: School Permissions,
Harcourt, Inc., 6277 Sea Harbor Drive, Orlando, Florida 32887-6777.

HARCOURT and the Harcourt Logo are trademarks of
Harcourt, Inc.

Printed in the United States of America

ISBN 0-15-321157-1

3 4 5 6 7 8 9 10 021 2003 2002

© Harcourt

What Are Living and Nonliving Things?

Read pages A5 to A7 in your textbook. Then read each question that follows. Decide which is the best answer to each question. Mark the space for your answer.

1. How are living things different from nonliving things?

   (A) Living things are tall. Nonliving things are short.

   (B) Living things are young. Nonliving things are old.

   (C) Living things need food, water, and air. Nonliving things do not.

   (D) Living things make noise. Nonliving things do not make noise.

2. Which is a living thing?

   (A) a rabbit
   (B) a pencil
   (C) a sled
   (D) a rock

3. Which is a nonliving thing?

   (A) a tree
   (B) a rosebush
   (C) a snake
   (D) a mountain

4. In this lesson, which of these is **NOT** a FACT about all living things?

   (A) All living things need food.

   (B) All living things need air.

   (C) All living things need light.

   (D) All living things need water.

© Harcourt

How Do Plants Grow and Change?

Read pages A9 to A13 in your textbook. Then read each question that follows. Decide which is the best answer to each question. Mark the space for your answer.

5. Which is **NOT** a FACT?

   (A) Flowers make seeds.

   (B) Roots use light to make food for a plant.

   (C) Stems move water through a plant.

   (D) Leaves use nutrients to make food for a plant.

6. The word <u>seedling</u> in this lesson means —

   (A) a plant that has seeds

   (B) a tiny seed

   (C) a young plant

   (D) an old plant

7. What does a seed do when it germinates?

   (A) It falls from the plant.

   (B) It dries up.

   (C) It freezes.

   (D) It starts to grow.

8. Look at this plant. Where is the sunlight coming from?

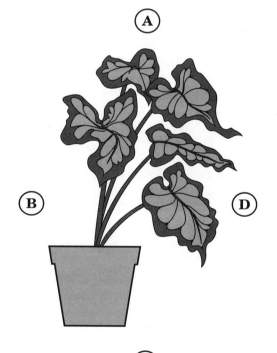

© Harcourt

How Are Plants Alike and Different?

Read pages A15 to A17 in your textbook. Then read each question that follows. Decide which is the best answer to each question. Mark the space for your answer.

9. A pine tree's leaves look like —

   (A) stars

   (B) acorns

   (C) eggs

   (D) needles

10. Where do acorns grow?

   (A) on oak trees

   (B) on pine trees

   (C) on maple trees

   (D) on cactuses

11. What is this lesson **MOSTLY** about?

   (A) Plants grow in the desert.

   (B) Plants are different from one another.

   (C) A pine cone protects its small, hard seeds.

   (D) A cactus plant grows flowers.

12. Why is a cactus able to live in the desert?

   (A) It doesn't need water.

   (B) Its flowers act like little umbrellas to protect it from the sun.

   (C) Its flowers have a lot of water.

   (D) It has very thick stems that store water.

© Harcourt

Write to Describe   Unit A, Chapter 1

A. Think about one of the plants you observed. Draw a picture of it.

B. Write two or three sentences about what you observed.

_____

_____

_____

_____

_____

_____

_____

© Harcourt

How Are Animals Alike and Different?

Read pages A25 to A29 in your textbook. Then read each question that follows. Decide which is the best answer to each question. Mark the space for your answer.

13. What is the **MOST** important idea of the paragraph on page A25?

    (A) Some animals have fur.

    (B) Animals use special body parts to fly.

    (C) There are many different kinds of animals.

    (D) All animals have some kind of body covering.

14. Mammals have —

    (A) feathers

    (B) smooth, wet skin

    (C) gills

    (D) fur or hair

15. Which is **NOT** a reptile?

    (A) a frog

    (B) a lizard

    (C) a turtle

    (D) a snake

16. Which animal does **NOT** have bones?

    (A) a chameleon

    (B) a turtle

    (C) a spider

    (D) a giraffe

© Harcourt

Name _____

What Are Some Animal Life Cycles?

Read pages A31 to A35 in your textbook. Then read each question that follows. Decide which is the best answer to each question. Mark the space for your answer.

17. Which of these happens second?

    (A) A chick grows inside an egg.

    (B) The chick gets too big for the egg.

    (C) A bird lays an egg.

    (D) The chick breaks the eggshell and hatches.

18. A <u>veterinarian</u> is a doctor for —

    (A) children

    (B) very old people

    (C) teeth

    (D) animals

19. Which sentence is **NOT** true?

    (A) Most bird parents take care of their chicks.

    (B) Goslings are baby geese.

    (C) Robins can fly as soon as they are born.

    (D) Robins get new feathers as they become adults.

20. Which set of arrows shows a cycle?

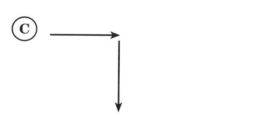

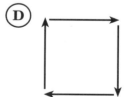

© Harcourt

Write to Describe   Unit A, Chapter 2

A. Think about the stages in the life cycle of a familiar animal.
    Draw pictures that show how the animal grows and changes.
    Write a sentence about each picture.

First stage, _____

Second stage, _____

Third stage, _____

B. Use another sheet of paper. Write a paragraph that describes the
    life cycle of the animal. Use your notes.

© Harcourt

How Will I Grow?

Read pages A43 to A47 in your textbook. Then read each question that follows. Decide which is the best answer to each question. Mark the space for your answer.

21. Which of these is **NOT** a FACT?

    Ⓐ When you are an adult, your body doesn't change.

    Ⓑ All people grow and change.

    Ⓒ As you get older, your skin will get wrinkles.

    Ⓓ Learning is a way to grow and change.

22. What are permanent teeth?

    Ⓐ teeth that grow in after your baby teeth fall out

    Ⓑ your two front top teeth

    Ⓒ the teeth that fall out

    Ⓓ a third set of teeth

23. Look at the paragraph on page A44. Which sentence tells the **MOST** important idea?

    Ⓐ First, you were a baby.

    Ⓑ Later on, you will be a teenager.

    Ⓒ All people grow and change.

    Ⓓ After that, you will become an adult.

24. Who is the oldest member of the family on pages A44 and A45?

    Ⓐ the 15-year-old son

    Ⓑ the mother

    Ⓒ the father

    Ⓓ the grandmother

© Harcourt

What Do My Bones and Muscles Do?

Read pages A49 to A53 in your textbook. Then read each question that follows. Decide which is the best answer to each question. Mark the space for your answer.

25. Which one is a muscle?

   (A) the spine

   (B) the ribs

   (C) the skull

   (D) the heart

26. Which of these is **NOT** true about muscles?

   (A) Your muscles are under your skin.

   (B) Your muscles work in pairs.

   (C) Your muscles move your bones.

   (D) You have about 75 muscles in your body.

27. Which of these bones protect your heart?

   (A) ribs

   (B) leg bones

   (C) arm bones

   (D) foot bones

28. What is your skeleton?

   (A) the bones that help you move

   (B) the bones that protect parts inside your body

   (C) all of your bones

   (D) the part of the body that protects your bones

© Harcourt

How Do My Heart and Lungs Work?

Read pages A55 to A59 in your textbook. Then read each question that follows. Decide which is the best answer to each question. Mark the space for your answer.

29. Which sentence is **TRUE**?

(A) Your heart looks like your fist.

(B) Your heart acts like a fist.

(C) Your heart is about the same size as your fist.

(D) Everyone's heart is the same size.

30. What happens after air moves down to your lungs?

(A) Your heart pumps blood to all parts of your body.

(B) Your blood picks up oxygen from your lungs.

(C) Your blood takes the oxygen to your heart.

(D) Your lungs take in oxygen from the air.

31. Rate in this lesson means —

(A) size

(B) shape

(C) speed

(D) sound

32. What happens when you breathe in?

(A) Your lungs get larger.

(B) Your lungs get smaller.

(C) Your heart beats faster.

(D) Your heart slows down.

© Harcourt

How Do I Digest Food?

Read pages A61 to A65 in your textbook. Then read each question that follows. Decide which is the best answer to each question. Mark the space for your answer.

33. The small intestine is connected to the —

    (A) stomach and large intestine

    (B) only the large intestine

    (C) only the stomach

    (D) stomach and the tube to the stomach

34. Which foods should you eat the **LEAST** of?

    (A) milk, yogurt, and cheese

    (B) meat and eggs

    (C) fats, oils, and sweets

    (D) dry beans and nuts

35. Which of these is **NOT** a group in the Food Guide Pyramid?

    (A) milk, yogurt, and cheese

    (B) fruits

    (C) bread, cereal, rice, and pasta

    (D) pizza, popcorn, and snacks

36. In this selection, <u>saliva</u> means —

    (A) the mouth

    (B) a bag of muscles that squeeze food

    (C) the liquid in your mouth that begins to break down food

    (D) the liquid food that moves into the small intestine

© Harcourt

Writing Practice

Write a Personal Story

Unit A, Chapter 3

A. Tell how some information or skill you have learned has helped you grow and change. Write your notes below.

What I learned: _____

_____

When I learned it: _____

_____

How I learned it (from a person? from a book? by myself?):

_____

B. Draw a picture to show yourself learning or doing this new thing.

© Harcourt

C. Use another sheet of paper. Write a story about what you learned and what happened afterwards. Use your notes to help you.

Unit A, Chapter 1

Choose the best answer. Then mark the space for the answer.

1. Jo planted an orange seed. About how long will it take for the seed to germinate? Mark your answer.

   Ⓐ more than 1 hour

   Ⓑ less than 1 hour

2. How long is the pine needle? Mark your answer.

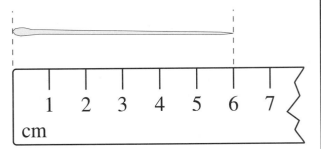

   Ⓐ 4 centimeters

   Ⓑ 5 centimeters

   Ⓒ 6 centimeters

   Ⓓ 7 centimeters

3. Mary has 5 walnuts and 3 pecans. Which number sentence shows how many nuts Mary has in all? Mark your answer.

   Ⓐ $5 - 3 = 2$

   Ⓑ $3 + 2 = 5$

   Ⓒ $3 \times 5 = 15$

   Ⓓ $5 + 3 = 8$

4. Which tool should you use to measure the length of a leaf? Mark your answer.

   Ⓐ

   Ⓑ

   Ⓒ

   Ⓓ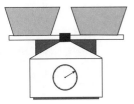

© Harcourt

Name_____

Unit A, Chapter 2

Math Practice

Choose the best answer. Then mark the space for the answer.

5. Which graph best shows the information in the tally table? Mark your answer.

KINDS OF PETS

Pet	Number of Pets
Mammal	II
Bird	II
Reptile	II
Amphibian	卌
Fish	III

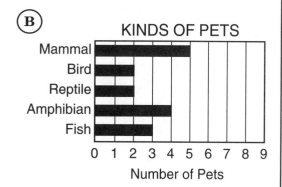

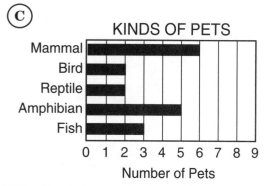

6. About how much does a cat weigh? Mark your answer.

   Ⓐ more than a pound

   Ⓑ less than a pound

7. Which insect is missing in the pattern? Mark your answer.

   Ⓐ

   Ⓑ

   Ⓒ

8. Carlos saw 5 snakes and 9 alligators at the zoo. How many reptiles did he see in all? Mark your answer.

   Ⓐ 11 reptiles

   Ⓑ 13 reptiles

   Ⓒ 14 reptiles

   Ⓓ 15 reptiles

© Harcourt

Name _____

Unit A, Chapter 3

Choose the best answer. Then mark the space for the answer.

9. The clock shows Andy that it is time for dinner. What time does the clock show? Mark your answer.

Ⓐ 5:15
Ⓑ 5:30
Ⓒ 5:45
Ⓓ 6:45

10. The spinner can stop on the heart, the lungs, or the skeleton. Which do you think it will stop on **MOST** often? Mark your answer.

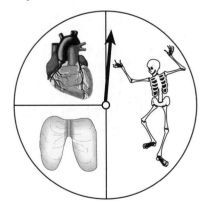

Ⓐ
Ⓑ
Ⓒ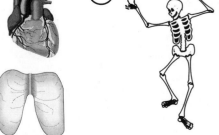

11. Tasha had 20 baby teeth. This year she lost 3 of them. Which shows how many baby teeth she has now? Mark your answer.

Ⓐ 20 + 3 = 23
Ⓑ 20 − 3 = 17
Ⓒ 17 + 2 = 19
Ⓓ 17 − 3 = 14

12. Use the graph to answer the question below.

FAVORITE EXERCISE

Exercise	Number of Children
Playing Sports	🧍🧍🧍🧍
Swimming	🧍
Running	🧍🧍🧍
Walking	🧍🧍

Each 🧍 stands for 2 children.

How many children like playing sports the best? Mark your answer.

Ⓐ 2 children
Ⓑ 3 children
Ⓒ 4 children
Ⓓ 8 children

Go On

Unit A, Chapter 3

Choose the best answer. Then mark the space for the answer.

13. There are 10 ladybugs on each of 3 leaves. There are 5 ladybugs on the ground. How many ladybugs are there in all? Mark your answer.

Tens	Ones

Ⓐ 13   Ⓒ 35

Ⓑ 15   Ⓓ 53

14. Which items are in order from lightest to heaviest? Mark your answer.

Ⓐ

Ⓑ

Ⓒ

Ⓓ

15. An ant has 3 body parts and 6 legs. How many legs do 3 ants have? Mark your answer.

Ⓐ 6 legs

Ⓑ 9 legs

Ⓒ 12 legs

Ⓓ 18 legs

16. Donna's heart beats 62 times in a minute. Karen's heart beats 70 times in a minute. How much faster is Karen's heart rate than Donna's? Mark your answer.

Ⓐ 2 beats a minute faster

Ⓑ 7 beats a minute faster

Ⓒ 8 beats a minute faster

Ⓓ 12 beats a minute faster

STOP

© Harcourt

Unit A, Review

Choose the best answer. Then mark the space for the answer.

17. How does your heart rate change when you exercise? Mark your answer.

   (A) Your heart rate gets faster.

   (B) Your heart rate gets slower.

   (C) Your heart rate stays the same.

18. Your wrist, palm, and fingers are part of your hand. There are 8 bones in your wrist, 5 bones in your palm, and 14 bones in your fingers. How many bones are in your hand? Mark your answer.

   (A) 19 bones

   (B) 22 bones

   (C) 26 bones

   (D) 27 bones

19. Patrick traces his shoe and his father's shoe. Patrick's shoe is 8 inches long. His father's shoe is 14 inches long. Which number sentence shows how much longer Patrick's father's shoe is than his own shoe? Mark your answer.

   (A) $14 - 8 = 6$

   (B) $14 - 6 = 8$

   (C) $8 + 6 = 14$

   (D) $8 - 6 = 2$

20. Which tool should you use to measure the length of a person's hand? Mark your answer.

   (A)

   (B)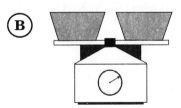

   (C) 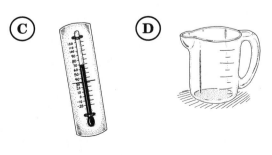 (D)

© Harcourt

Name _____

How Do People Use Rocks and Soil?

Read pages B5 to B9 in your textbook. Then read each question that follows. Decide which is the best answer to each question. Mark the space for your answer.

1. What is Mount Rushmore?

   Ⓐ a volcano

   Ⓑ a sculpture carved out of a mountain

   Ⓒ the place where four presidents lived

   Ⓓ the name of a town

2. According to the picture on page B6, the surface of an obsidian rock is —

   Ⓐ dull

   Ⓑ shiny

   Ⓒ rough

   Ⓓ light-colored

3. Which of these is **NOT** a kind of soil?

   Ⓐ topsoil

   Ⓑ clay soil

   Ⓒ adobe

   Ⓓ sandy soil

4. Look at the picture on page B8. Which soil holds the **MOST** water?

   Ⓐ clay soil

   Ⓑ topsoil

   Ⓒ sandy soil

   Ⓓ none of them

© Harcourt

Name ________________________________ Reading Comprehension

How Do People Use Water?

Read pages B11 to B13 in your textbook. Then read each question that follows. Decide which is the best answer to each question. Mark the space for your answer.

5. What is one way people use water for transportation?
   - (A) watering a flower garden
   - (B) sailing a boat
   - (C) washing their cars
   - (D) washing their clothes

6. In this lesson, <u>transportation</u> means —
   - (A) ways to move people or things
   - (B) the flow of the river
   - (C) ways to make electricity
   - (D) boats and ships

7. Water makes electricity when the flow of the river —
   - (A) moves boats and ships
   - (B) is stopped by a dam
   - (C) turns machines
   - (D) washes clothes

8. People, plants, and animals need water —
   - (A) to make electricity
   - (B) to wash dishes
   - (C) to cook
   - (D) to live and grow

© Harcourt

What Other Natural Resources Do People Use?

Read pages B15 to B19 in your textbook. Then read each question that follows. Decide which is the best answer to each question. Mark the space for your answer.

9. What are some ways people use plants?

   (A) for making coins

   (B) for making cloth and clothing

   (C) for breaking big rocks

   (D) for blowing bubbles

10. Which one is **NOT** a mineral?

   (A) soap

   (B) iron

   (C) topaz

   (D) diamond

11. Who is using air?

   (A) Matty is riding a roller coaster.

   (B) Della is putting on sunscreen.

   (C) José is blowing up a balloon.

   (D) Bud is tying his sneakers.

12. What happens last when paper is made?

   (A) The pulp is pressed flat to make sheets.

   (B) A tree is cut down.

   (C) Wood chips are made into pulp.

   (D) A pine stool is made.

© Harcourt

Name _____

Write to Describe   Unit B, Chapter 1

A.   Think about a resource. Draw people using this resource.

B.   Write notes about the resource.

   1   What type of resource is it?

   _____

   2   How is it used?

   _____

   _____

   _____

C.   Use another sheet of paper. Write a paragraph that describes this
      resource. Use your drawing and notes to help you.

© Harcourt

What Is a Fossil?

Read pages B27 to B31 in your textbook. Then read each question that follows. Decide which is the best answer to each question. Mark the space for your answer.

13. A fish becomes a fossil over many years. First, the fish dies. What is the second thing that happens?

   Ⓐ The print of the fish is left in the rock.

   Ⓑ The fish's body sinks to the ocean floor.

   Ⓒ The fish's body rots.

   Ⓓ The mud turns to rock.

14. What is the name for the hard sap of pine trees?

   Ⓐ a fossil

   Ⓑ amber

   Ⓒ tar

   Ⓓ prints

15. Look at the picture of the mammoth fossil on page B31. What can we tell about the mammoth from looking at its fossil?

   Ⓐ It had long, brown fur.

   Ⓑ It had very good eye sight.

   Ⓒ It had long tusks.

   Ⓓ It ran fast.

16. A paleontologist is —

   Ⓐ an artist who draws pictures of fossils

   Ⓑ a mechanic who builds electronic dinosaurs

   Ⓒ an artist who makes sculptures of dinosaurs

   Ⓓ a scientist who finds and studies fossils

© Harcourt

How Do Scientists Get Fossils?

Read pages B33 to B35 in your textbook. Then read each question that follows. Decide which is the best answer to each question. Mark the space for your answer.

17. Putting a fossil together is a lot like —

   (A) putting together a jigsaw puzzle

   (B) baking a cake

   (C) playing a board game

   (D) taking apart a radio

18. What is the first thing scientists do after they bring a fossil to the museum?

   (A) put it on display

   (B) set all the pieces out on a big table

   (C) glue the pieces together

   (D) clean the pieces

19. How do scientists get fossils out of rock?

   (A) They soak the rock in water until the fossils wash out.

   (B) They carefully chip away at the rock until they free the fossil.

   (C) They break up the rock with hammers.

   (D) They soak the rock in acid.

20. In this lesson, reconstruct means —

   (A) rebuild

   (B) sell

   (C) fix

   (D) paint

© Harcourt

What Have Scientists Learned About Dinosaurs?

Read pages B37 to B41 in your textbook. Then read each question that follows. Decide which is the best answer to each question. Mark the space for your answer.

21. Look at the dinosaur graph on pages B38 and B39. About how tall was a Stegosaurus?

    (A) about 4 feet

    (B) about 10 feet

    (C) about 12 feet

    (D) about 16 feet

22. What does the word <u>dinosaur</u> mean?

    (A) tyrant lizard king

    (B) three-horned face

    (C) fierce ruler

    (D) terrible lizard

23. What will fossils NOT tell scientists?

    (A) what dinosaur skin looked like

    (B) what dinosaurs ate

    (C) how tall dinosaurs were

    (D) what color dinosaurs were

24. What did scientists learn when they studied the teeth of Triceratops?

    (A) Triceratops did not have any cavities.

    (B) Triceratops grew a new set of teeth every few years.

    (C) Its teeth were flat like the teeth of today's plant-eating animals.

    (D) Triceratops swallowed its food without chewing it.

© Harcourt

Write to Inform   Unit B, Chapter 2

A. What are four facts you think everyone should know about dinosaurs? Write notes or make a drawing about each fact in the chart below.

Fact 1: _____

_____

Fact 2: _____

_____

Fact 3: _____

_____

Fact 4: _____

_____

B. Use another sheet of paper. Write one or more paragraphs to tell others about dinosaurs. Use your notes or drawings to help you.

© Harcourt

Unit B, Chapter 1

Choose the best answer. Then mark the space for the answer.

1. Which rock has a mass greater than the mass of the box of crayons? Mark your answer.

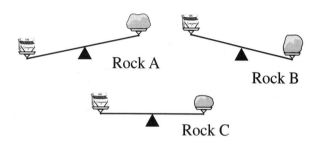

Rock A

Rock B

Rock C

  Ⓐ   Rock A

  Ⓑ   Rock B

  Ⓒ   Rock C

2. About how long is the rock? Mark your answer.

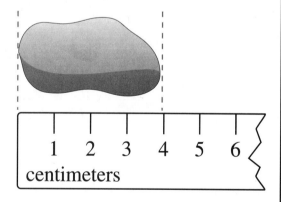

centimeters

  Ⓐ   1 centimeter

  Ⓑ   2 centimeters

  Ⓒ   3 centimeters

  Ⓓ   4 centimeters

3. What is the temperature? Mark your answer.

  Ⓐ   40°F

  Ⓑ   45°F

  Ⓒ   50°F

  Ⓓ   55°F

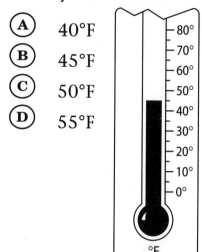

4. Ann started to make a bird feeder at

She finished 15 minutes later. What time did she finish? Mark your answer.

  Ⓐ   4:15

  Ⓑ   4:30

  Ⓒ   4:45

  Ⓓ   5:00

Go On

© Harcourt

Unit B, Chapter 1

Choose the best answer. Then mark the space for the answer.

Use the tally table to answer Questions 5 and 6.

How Our Class Uses Water in One Day

Uses of Water	How Many Times
Drinking	卌 卌 |||
Washing hands	卌 卌	
Watering plants	|||
Cleaning	卌

5. How many more times did the class use water for washing hands than for cleaning? Mark your answer.

(A) 3
(B) 4
(C) 5
(D) 6

6. Which way did the class use water **MOST**? Mark your answer.

(A) cleaning
(B) washing hands
(C) drinking
(D) watering plants

7. Are you more likely to pull a picture of an apple or grapes from the bag? Mark your answer.

(A) apple
(B) grapes

8. It takes 2 cups of water to brush your teeth. There are 5 people in the family. How many cups of water does the family use in all? Mark your answer.

(A) 4 cups
(B) 6 cups
(C) 8 cups
(D) 10 cups

STOP

© Harcourt

Unit B, Chapter 2

Math Practice

Choose the best answer. Then mark the space for the answer.

9. Jared has 13 plant fossils and 6 animal fossils. How many fossils does Jared have in all? Mark your answer.

(A) 9

(B) 19

(C) 21

(D) 29

10. About how many rocks are in the jar? Mark your answer.

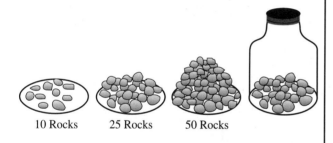

10 Rocks   25 Rocks   50 Rocks

(A) about 5

(B) about 10

(C) about 25

(D) about 50

11. How long is this fossil? Mark your answer.

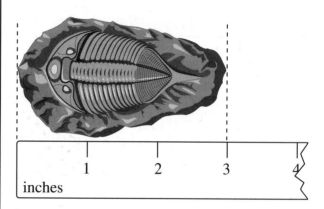

(A) 2 inches

(B) 3 inches

(C) 4 inches

(D) 5 inches

12. How much longer was the Stegosaurus than Scelidosaurus? Mark your answer.

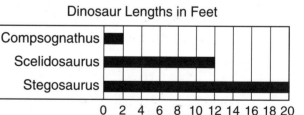

Dinosaur Lengths in Feet

(A) 4 feet   (C) 8 feet

(B) 6 feet   (D) 10 feet

Go On

© Harcourt

Unit B, Chapter 2

Choose the best answer. Then mark the space for the answer.

Use the graph to answer Questions 13 and 14.

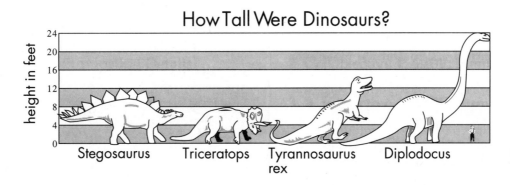

How Tall Were Dinosaurs?

13. Which dinosaur was the tallest? Mark your answer.

Ⓐ Stegosaurus
Ⓑ Triceratops
Ⓒ Tyrannosaurus rex
Ⓓ Diplodocus

14. Which list shows the dinosaurs in order from shortest to tallest? Mark your answer.

Ⓐ Diplodocus, Triceratops, Tyrannosaurus rex, Stegosaurus
Ⓑ Triceratops, Tyrannosaurus rex, Stegosaurus, Diplodocus
Ⓒ Triceratops, Stegosaurus, Tyrannosaurus rex, Diplodocus
Ⓓ Stegosaurus, Diplodocus, Tyrannosaurus rex, Triceratops

15. Which object is less than 1 foot long? Mark your answer.

Ⓐ baseball bat
Ⓑ car
Ⓒ key
Ⓓ bicycle

16. Choose the reasonable answer. A scientist found 32 dinosaur fossils in Colorado and 27 dinosaur fossils in Montana. How many fossils did she find in all? Mark your answer.

Ⓐ 55
Ⓑ 59
Ⓒ 68
Ⓓ 69

© Harcourt

Math Practice

Unit B, Review

Choose the best answer. Then mark the space for the answer.

17. Which tool should you use to measure how long a fossil is? Mark your answer.

Ⓐ

Ⓑ

Ⓒ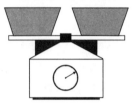

Ⓓ

18. The paleontologist found 5 fossils in tar, 8 fossils in rock, and 3 fossils in amber. How many fossils did the paleontologist find in all? Mark your answer.

Ⓐ 13

Ⓑ 14

Ⓒ 15

Ⓓ 16

19. Paul has 4 marble rocks and 8 lava rocks. Which number sentence shows how many rocks he has in all? Mark your answer.

Ⓐ 4 + 4 = 8

Ⓑ 8 + 8 = 16

Ⓒ 4 + 8 = 12

Ⓓ 8 − 4 = 4

20. Scelidosaurus was about 12 feet long. Compsognathus was about 2 feet long. About how much longer was Scelidosaurus than Compsognathus? Mark your answer.

Ⓐ about 1 foot

Ⓑ about 10 feet

Ⓒ about 11 feet

Ⓓ about 14 feet

© Harcourt

What Is Matter?

Read pages C5 to C7 in your textbook. Then read each question that follows. Decide which is the best answer to each question. Mark the space for your answer.

1. In this lesson, <u>matter</u> is —
   - (A) what all things are made of
   - (B) the space something takes up
   - (C) the mass of something
   - (D) the color, size, and shape of things

2. What is the **MOST** important idea of the paragraph on page C6?
   - (A) A chair is a solid.
   - (B) Matter has three forms: solid, liquid, and gas.
   - (C) Matter has certain properties.
   - (D) The air in a balloon is a gas.

3. The juice on page C6 is an example of a —
   - (A) solid
   - (B) gas
   - (C) solid and gas
   - (D) liquid

4. Which sentence tells a property of the chair on page C6?
   - (A) No one is sitting on it.
   - (B) It is on the floor.
   - (C) It is orange.
   - (D) It is from the kindergarten room.

© Harcourt

What Can We Find Out About Solids?

Read pages C9 to C13 in your textbook. Then read each question that follows. Decide which is the best answer to each question. Mark the space for your answer.

5. Look at the chart on page C13. The box is —

   (A) longer than the wood

   (B) shorter than the wood

   (C) heavier than the wood

   (D) the same size as the wood

6. What property of the crayons on page C11 makes them different from one another?

   (A) length

   (B) shape

   (C) use

   (D) color

7. Ben grouped some of the objects on pages C10 and C11. Here is the chart he made. Which object does not belong?

   Things that have bumps on them

   (A) twig

   (B) dinosaur

   (C) baseball

   (D) paper clip

8. A <u>centimeter</u> is a unit used to measure —

   (A) weight

   (B) length

   (C) mass

   (D) size

© Harcourt

What Can We Find Out About Liquids?

Read pages C15 to C19 in your textbook. Then read each question that follows. Decide which is the best answer to each question. Mark the space for your answer.

9. Which is **NOT** true?

   (A) Liquids have mass.

   (B) Liquids have volume.

   (C) Liquids do not change in amount unless you add more or take some away.

   (D) Liquids have shape.

10. If you pour juice into a bottle, it will —

   (A) change in amount

   (B) take the shape of the bottle

   (C) keep its shape

   (D) take up less space

11. Look at this measuring cup. Which arrow points to 125 milliliters?

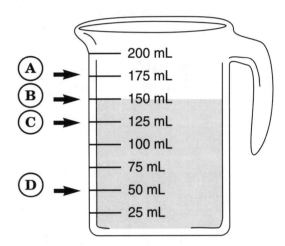

12. A <u>milliliter</u> is a unit used to measure —

   (A) weight

   (B) height

   (C) volume

   (D) mass

© Harcourt

What Can We Find Out About Gases?

Read pages C21 to C25 in your textbook. Then read each question that follows. Decide which is the best answer to each question. Mark the space for your answer.

13. How is a gas like a liquid?

- (A) It has no mass.
- (B) You can see through it.
- (C) It takes the shape of its container.
- (D) It fills all the space inside a container.

14. What did Garrett Morgan invent?

- (A) the hot-air balloon
- (B) the gas mask
- (C) the air pump
- (D) the gas grill

15. Look at the rod the girl is holding on pages C24 and C25. Suppose you took off the balloon filled with air and taped the yellow balloon in its place. What would happen?

- (A) The rod would tilt the same way it is tilting now.
- (B) The rod would tilt the other way.
- (C) The balloon would begin to rise.
- (D) The rod would begin to turn.

16. Which of these is an OPINION about air?

- (A) It fills the space of its container.
- (B) It is made up of gases.
- (C) It can lift a kite.
- (D) It feels good when it blows on me.

© Harcourt

Name _____

● Write to Explain   Unit C, Chapter 1

A. Draw a picture that shows people outdoors. Show all three forms of matter.

```



```

B. Write one or more sentences about each form of matter you show in your picture.

Solid: _____

_____

Liquid: _____

_____

Gas: _____

_____

© Harcourt

What Happens When You Mix Matter?

Read pages C33 to C37 in your textbook. Then read each question that follows. Decide which is the best answer to each question. Mark the space for your answer.

17. How could you change the mass of the loaf of bread on page C34?

Ⓐ Cut each slice in half.

Ⓑ Cut the rest of the bread into slices.

Ⓒ Arrange the slices so they form a different shape.

Ⓓ Eat a slice.

18. Which of these is a mixture?

Ⓐ peas

Ⓑ carrots

Ⓒ corn

Ⓓ rice and beans

19. Which is **NOT** an example of solid matter?

Ⓐ an orange

Ⓑ an orange crayon

Ⓒ orange juice

Ⓓ an orange tree

20. Which of these is **NOT** a FACT from the lesson?

Ⓐ Cutting is one way to change matter.

Ⓑ Changing the shape of matter changes its mass.

Ⓒ A mixture is made up of two or more things.

Ⓓ Matter can be cut and mixed.

© Harcourt

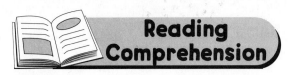
How Can Water Change?

Read pages C39 to C43 in your textbook. Then read each question that follows. Decide which is the best answer to each question. Mark the space for your answer.

21 Water as a solid may be —

(A) ice

(B) water vapor

(C) a puddle

(D) rain

22 What happens after water boils?

(A) It turns into a solid.

(B) It melts.

(C) It begins to evaporate.

(D) It condenses.

23 If the temperature goes above 0°C, ice —

(A) boils

(B) melts

(C) evaporates

(D) condenses

24 <u>Reversible</u> in this lesson means —

(A) not able to change back to the way it was

(B) not able to change from solid to liquid

(C) able to change back to the way it was

(D) not able to change from vapor to liquid

© Harcourt

What Other Ways Does Matter Change?

Read pages C45 to C49 in your textbook. Then read each question that follows. Decide which is the best answer to each question. Mark the space for your answer.

25. Which step in making gelatin happens last?

    (A) The hot liquid mixture begins to cool.

    (B) The gelatin powder is mixed with hot water.

    (C) The gelatin becomes firm.

    (D) The solid gelatin powder is put into a bowl.

26. Which change is reversible?

    (A) toasting a marshmallow

    (B) cooking a hamburger

    (C) mashing potatoes

    (D) mixing raisins in your cereal

27. Which change is irreversible?

    (A) scrambling an egg

    (B) folding a sheet of paper

    (C) turning on a light

    (D) bending a stick into the shape of a heart

28. An uncooked egg is one that is not cooked. What does the word part un- mean?

    (A) hot

    (B) mixed

    (C) not

    (D) hard

© Harcourt

Name _____

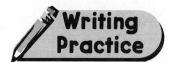

● Write to Describe Unit C, Chapter 2

A. Think about how water changes from a solid to a liquid to a
gas. Write notes to describe what happens. Draw pictures to
show the process.

Solid

First,

Liquid

Next,

Gas

Last,

B. Use another sheet of paper. Write a paragraph that describes how
water changes from a solid to a liquid to a gas. Use your notes.

© Harcourt

What Are Forces?

Read pages C59 to C65 in your textbook. Then read each question that follows. Decide which is the best answer to each question. Mark the space for your answer.

29. Which tells you something's location?

Ⓐ under the couch

Ⓑ running around

Ⓒ speaking softly

Ⓓ in a little while

30. The force that pulls things toward the center of Earth is called —

Ⓐ wind

Ⓑ magnetism

Ⓒ gravity

Ⓓ electricity

31. Wind is —

Ⓐ clouds

Ⓑ moving air

Ⓒ warm air

Ⓓ cold weather

32. Which of these is **NOT** an example of a force?

Ⓐ magnetism

Ⓑ moving water

Ⓒ location

Ⓓ pushing a ball

© Harcourt

How Can We Measure Motion?

Read pages C67 to C71 in your textbook. Then read each question that follows. Decide which is the best answer to each question. Mark the space for your answer.

33. Which of these is a FACT from the lesson?

Ⓐ It takes less force to move something heavy than something light.

Ⓑ It takes more force to move something a long distance than a short distance.

Ⓒ It takes less force to move something over a rough surface than over a smooth surface.

Ⓓ It takes more force to move something little than something big.

34. When something is in motion, it —

Ⓐ is moving

Ⓑ stays still

Ⓒ is a force

Ⓓ is going a long way

35. Daria wants to do the experiment shown on page C71. She made a list of the things she will need, but she left something out. What was it?

Things Used to Measure Force	
1. cardboard	4. paper clip
2. stapler	5. rubber band
3. book	6. string

Ⓐ a tape measure

Ⓑ staples

Ⓒ tape

Ⓓ a marker

36. Which of these is **NOT** a measure of motion?

Ⓐ how far something goes

Ⓑ how much time something takes to go from one spot to another

Ⓒ how much force it takes to pull something

Ⓓ how much friction there is

© Harcourt

Write to Inform Unit C, Chapter 3

A. List topics about force and motion that you might like to write a paragraph about.

_____

_____

_____

_____

_____

_____

_____

_____

B. Choose one topic. Write notes for your paragraph.

Topic:

_____

Detail:

_____

Detail:

_____

C. Use another sheet of paper. Write a paragraph using your notes.

© Harcourt

What Is Sound?

Read pages C79 to C83 in your textbook. Then read each question that follows. Decide which is the best answer to each question. Mark the space for your answer.

37. What is an <u>audiologist</u>?

   Ⓐ a teacher

   Ⓑ someone who tests people's hearing

   Ⓒ someone who tests sound equipment

   Ⓓ a heart doctor

38. You make sounds using your —

   Ⓐ eyes

   Ⓑ ears

   Ⓒ ribs

   Ⓓ vocal cords

39. How are your eardrums and vocal cords alike?

   Ⓐ They have the same shape.

   Ⓑ They are both in your throat.

   Ⓒ They both vibrate.

   Ⓓ They both help you make sounds.

40. In this lesson, <u>vibrate</u> means —

   Ⓐ let you hear

   Ⓑ move in every direction

   Ⓒ move back and forth very fast

   Ⓓ move slowly

© Harcourt

How Do Sounds Vary?

Read pages C85 to C87 in your textbook. Then read each question that follows. Decide which is the best answer to each question. Mark the space for your answer.

41. Which of these is a FACT from the lesson?

    (A) Sounds are all the same.

    (B) It takes more energy to make a high sound than a low sound.

    (C) Sounds are all around you.

    (D) You can see all sounds.

42. Which of these is **NOT** a FACT from the lesson?

    (A) It takes more energy to make a soft sound than a loud sound.

    (B) Sounds are different in loudness.

    (C) Sounds are different in pitch.

    (D) A bullfrog's croak is an example of a low-pitched sound.

43. In this lesson, <u>pitch</u> means —

    (A) how loud or soft a sound is

    (B) how high or low a sound is

    (C) how much energy a sound has

    (D) how different sounds are heard

44. Which of these is an example of a loud sound?

    (A) a person whispering

    (B) a bee buzzing

    (C) a person turning the pages of a book

    (D) a person shouting

© Harcourt

How Does Sound Travel?

Read pages C89 to C93 in your textbook. Then read each question that follows. Decide which is the best answer to each question. Mark the space for your answer.

45. What is the **MOST** important idea of the two paragraphs on page C91?

Ⓐ The air makes the cup vibrate.

Ⓑ The cup makes the string vibrate.

Ⓒ Sounds can travel through solid objects.

Ⓓ A person talks into one cup, making the air inside vibrate.

46. Sounds can travel through —

Ⓐ only gases and solids

Ⓑ only gases and liquids

Ⓒ only gases

Ⓓ gases, solids, and liquids

47. Sonar in this lesson means —

Ⓐ a way to find things that are lost

Ⓑ a way to use sounds to locate things under water

Ⓒ a way to use sounds to locate things in space

Ⓓ the way whales talk to each other

48. Which of these is an example of sound traveling through solids?

Ⓐ a person hearing a bell ring

Ⓑ people talking through a string telephone

Ⓒ dolphins locating objects

Ⓓ whales communicating

© Harcourt

Name _____

Reading Comprehension

How Can We Make Different Sounds?

Read pages C95 to C97 in your textbook. Then read each question that follows. Decide which is the best answer to each question. Mark the space for your answer.

49. The faster a string vibrates, the —

(A) higher the sound

(B) lower the sound

(C) longer the sound

(D) shorter the sound

50. Look at the picture on page C96. How is the boy's cup like a musical instrument?

(A) They have the same shape.

(B) They are both made of metal.

(C) You can produce sound by blowing into them.

(D) They both have strings.

51. This lesson tells you about all of the following EXCEPT —

(A) how to give a stringed instrument a higher sound

(B) how to make a drum sound softer

(C) the difference between thin strings and thick strings

(D) how dolphins communicate

52. Which of these is NOT a FACT from the lesson?

(A) You cannot change the loudness of a sound.

(B) Hitting a drum with a lot of energy makes a loud sound.

(C) Tapping a drum lightly makes a soft sound.

(D) Some musical instruments have strings.

© Harcourt

46   Harcourt Science California Standardized Test Preparation   Unit C • Chapter 4 • Use with Lesson 4.

Write to Describe Unit C, Chapter 4

A. List different living and nonliving things that make sounds.

_____

_____

_____

_____

_____

_____

B. Choose one thing you listed to write about. Write its name in the circle below. On the lines that extend from the circle, write some words to describe the sound the thing makes and how you can change the sound.

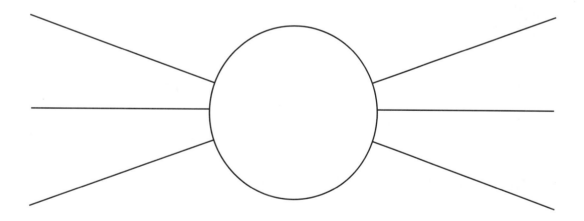

C. On a separate sheet of paper, write a paragraph about the thing you chose. Describe the sound that it makes and ways you can change that sound.

© Harcourt

Name_____

Unit C, Chapter 1

Math Practice

Choose the best answer. Then mark the space for the answer.

1. Which unit is used to measure length? Mark your answer.

   (A) milliliter
   (B) centimeter
   (C) cup
   (D) degree

2. Which lists the animals in order from least mass to greatest mass? Mark your answer.

   (A) bird, raccoon, elephant
   (B) elephant, raccoon, bird
   (C) raccoon, bird, elephant
   (D) bird, elephant, raccoon

3. About how long is this piece of chalk? Mark your answer.

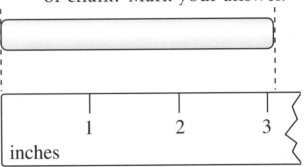

   (A) 1 inch
   (B) 2 inches
   (C) 3 inches
   (D) 4 inches

4. Which tool should you use to measure the amount of water in a glass? Mark your answer.

   (A)
   (B)
   (C) 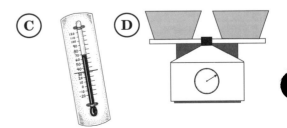 (D)

© Harcourt

Unit C • Use with Chapter 1.

Unit C, Chapter 2

Choose the best answer. Then mark the space for the answer.

5. Are you more likely to pull a picture of a puffy cloud or a flat cloud? Mark your answer.

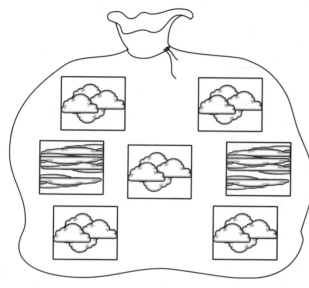

 A   B

puffy   flat

6. An apple slice had a mass of 4 units. After the slice dried, the slice had a mass of 2 units. Which shows how much mass the apple slice lost? Mark your answer.

Ⓐ   2 + 2 = 4

Ⓑ   4 + 2 = 6

Ⓒ   6 − 4 = 2

Ⓓ   4 − 2 = 2

7. Dan put 8 paper clips, 5 tacks, 6 rubber bands on one side of a balance. How many objects did he put on that side of the balance? Mark your answer.

Ⓐ   17

Ⓑ   18

Ⓒ   19

Ⓓ   20

8. Choose the reasonable answer.

Ann counted 56 almonds and 37 peanuts in her snack mixture. How many almonds and peanuts were there in all? Mark your answer.

Ⓐ   93

Ⓑ   193

Ⓒ   390

Ⓓ   930

© Harcourt

Unit C, Chapter 3

Math Practice

Choose the best answer. Then mark the space for the answer.

9. Pat used a force of 200. Sally used a force of 75. Who used the greatest force? Mark your answer.

(A) Sally

(B) Pat

10. The scale in the pictures below measures the amount of force used by each person.

Picture A

Picture B

Which picture shows the greater force? Mark your answer.

(A) Picture A

(B) Picture B

The stronger the magnet, the more paper clips it can attract at the same time.

Use the table to answer Questions 11 and 12.

Magnet	Number of Paper Clips Attracted
A	7
B	3
C	5

11. Which magnet is the strongest? Mark your answer.

(A) Magnet A

(B) Magnet B

(C) Magnet C

12. An even stronger magnet attracts as many paper clips as Magnet A, Magnet B, and Magnet C together. How many paper clips in all does the stronger magnet attract? Mark your answer.

(A) 8   (C) 12

(B) 10   (D) 15

© Harcourt

Math Practice

Unit C, Chapter 4

Choose the best answer. Then mark the space for the answer.

Use the pictures below to answer Questions 13 and 14.

13. When you pour water into bottles and then tap the bottles, you hear sounds. The less water there is in the bottle, the higher the pitch of the sound is.

1 2 3 4 5 6

Which bottle will have the highest pitch? Mark your answer.

(A) Bottle 2 (C) Bottle 5
(B) Bottle 4 (D) Bottle 6

14. Which two bottles will have the same pitch? Mark your answer.

(A) Bottles 1 and 3
(B) Bottles 2 and 3
(C) Bottles 4 and 5
(D) Bottles 5 and 6

15. Jack did not hear the alarm clock ring at

Jack got out of bed when the alarm clock rang again 15 minutes later. What time did Jack get out of bed? Mark your answer.

(A) 7:30 (C) 8:00
(B) 7:45 (D) 8:15

16. Ross made 4 guitars. He used 3 rubber bands for each guitar. How many rubber bands did he use in all? Mark your answer.

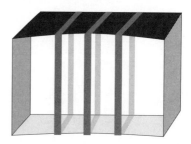

(A) 8 (C) 12
(B) 10 (D) 14

© Harcourt

Unit C, Review

Choose the best answer. Then mark the space for the answer.

17. About how long is the pen? Mark your answer.

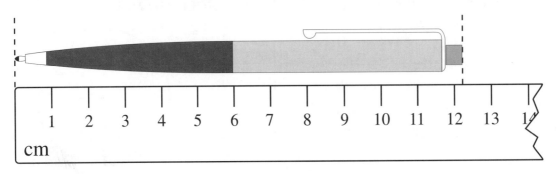

Ⓐ 11 centimeters   Ⓒ 13 centimeters

Ⓑ 12 centimeters   Ⓓ 14 centimeters

18. How much water is in the measuring cup? Mark your answer.

Ⓐ 75 milliliters

Ⓑ 100 milliliters

Ⓒ 150 milliliters

Ⓓ 175 milliliters

19. Bob pushed two toy cars. Car A went 30 centimeters. Car B went 55 centimeters. Which car was given a harder push? Mark your answer.

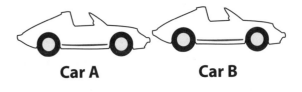

Car A   Car B

Ⓐ Car A   Ⓑ Car B

20. Less force is needed to move light objects and more force is needed to move heavy objects. Which object takes the **MOST** force to move? Mark your answer.

Ⓐ spoon   Ⓒ stove

Ⓑ pan   Ⓓ radio

© Harcourt